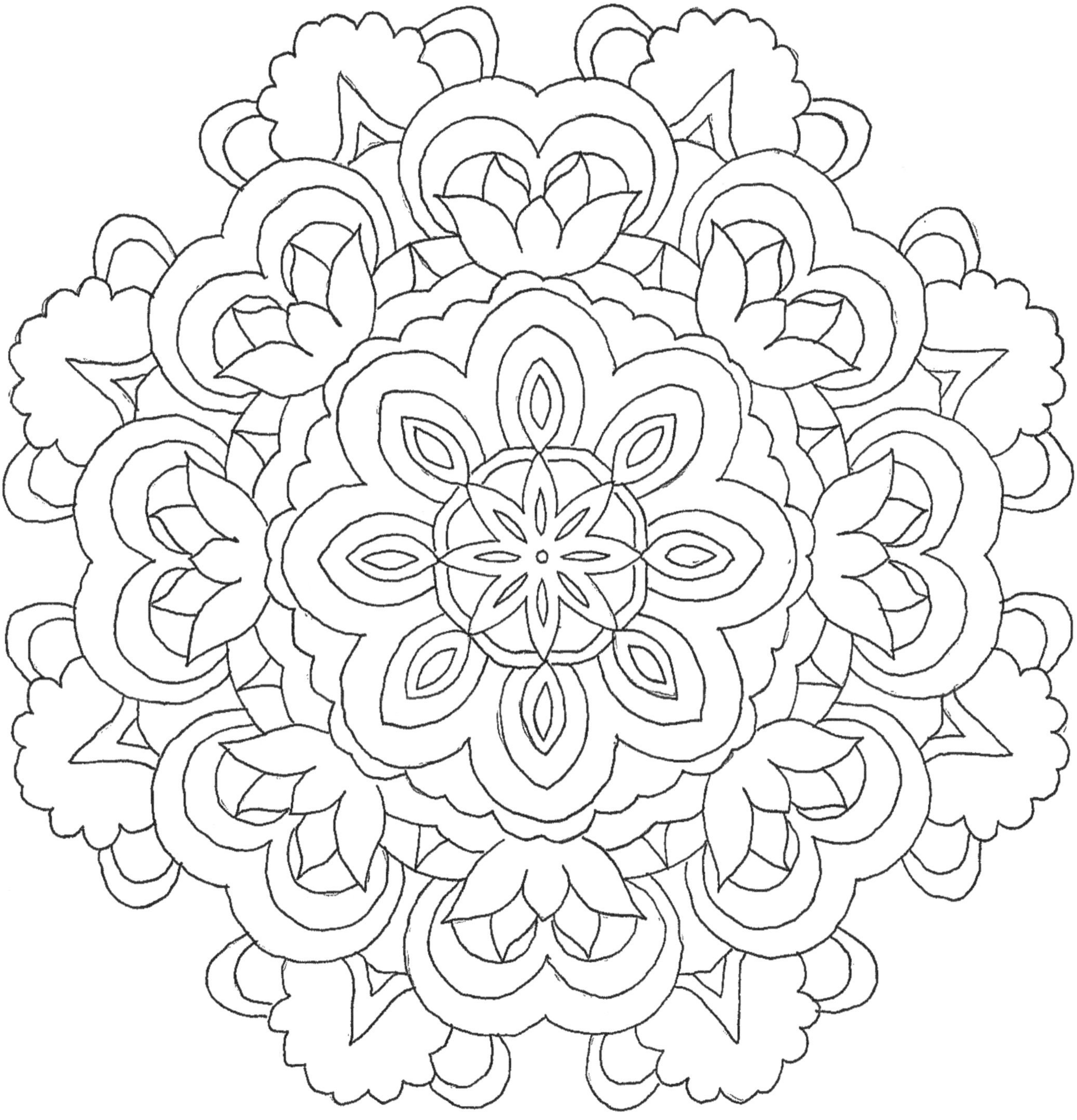

List things you would like to hear from others.

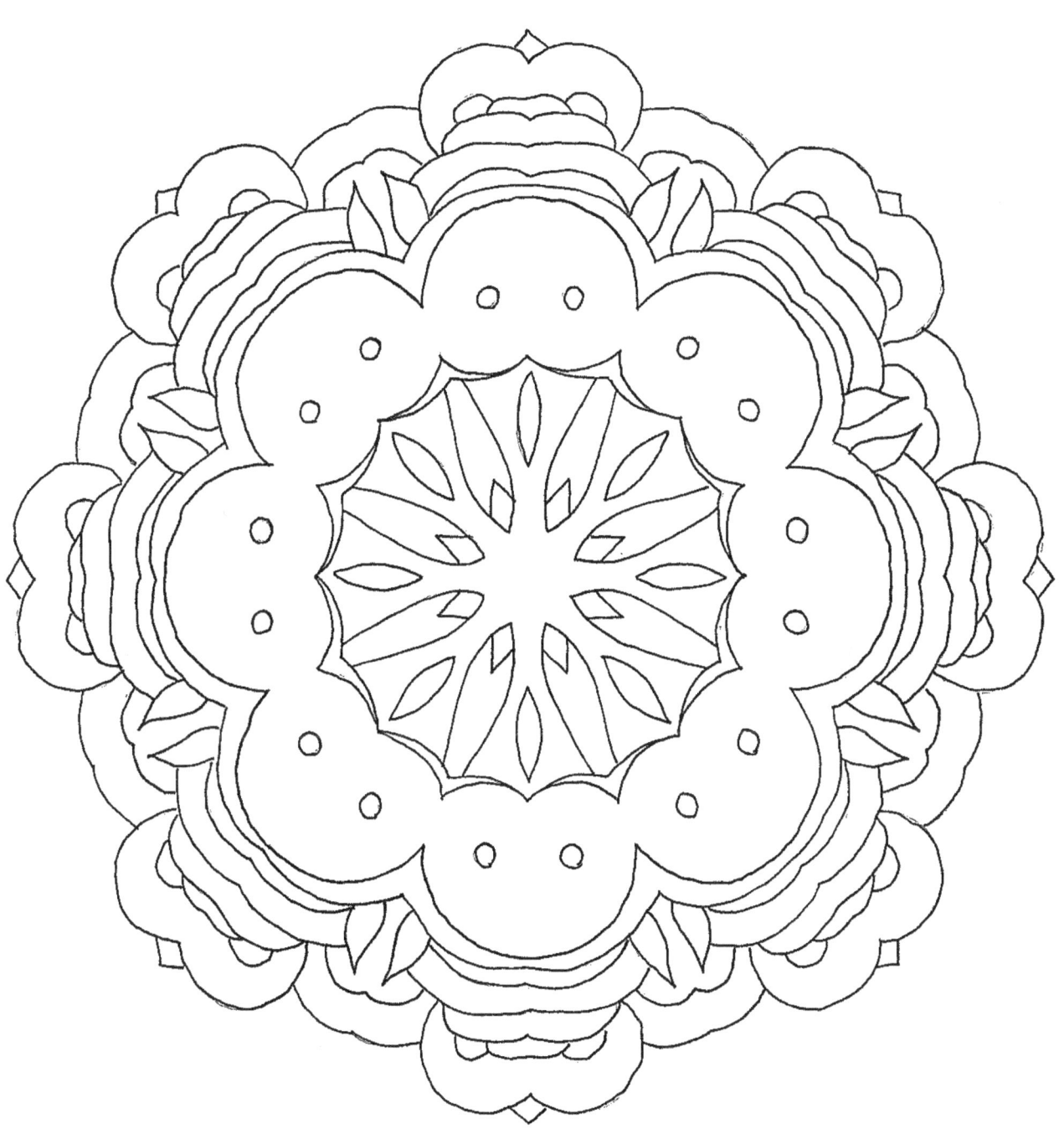

Write things that used to scare you but don't any more.

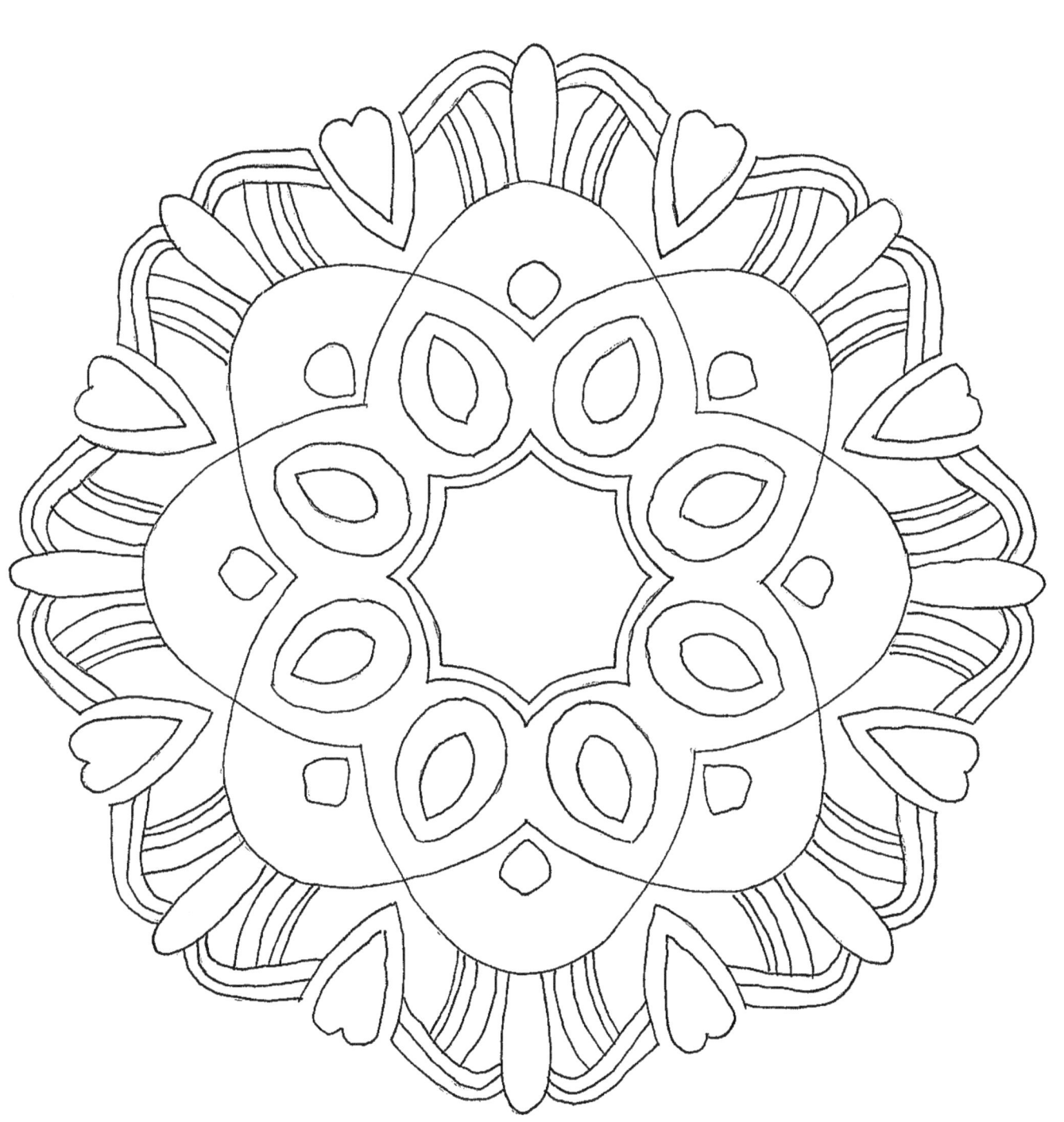

List ways you sabotage yourself in your journal.

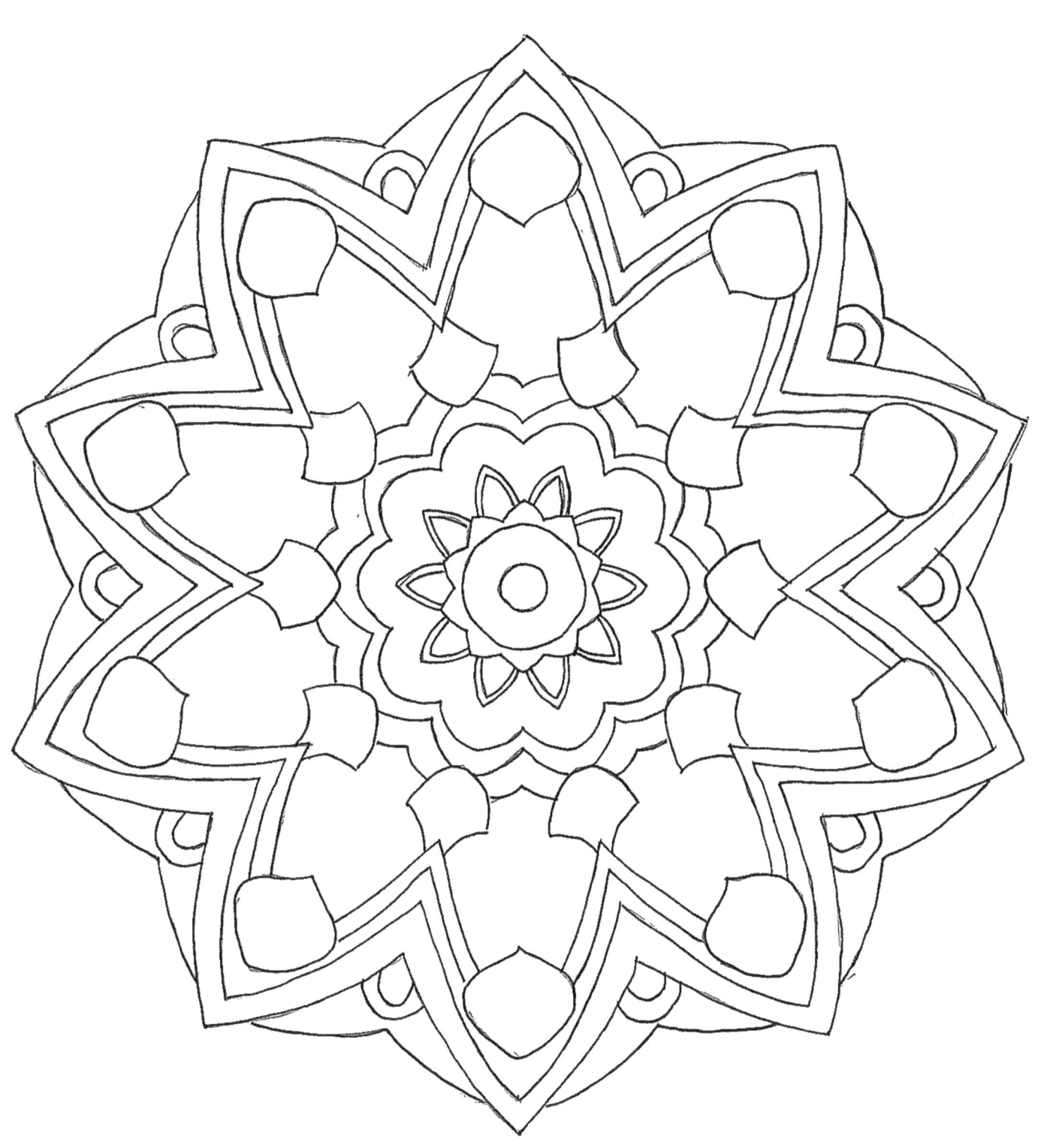

Make a list of things you are sad or angry about.

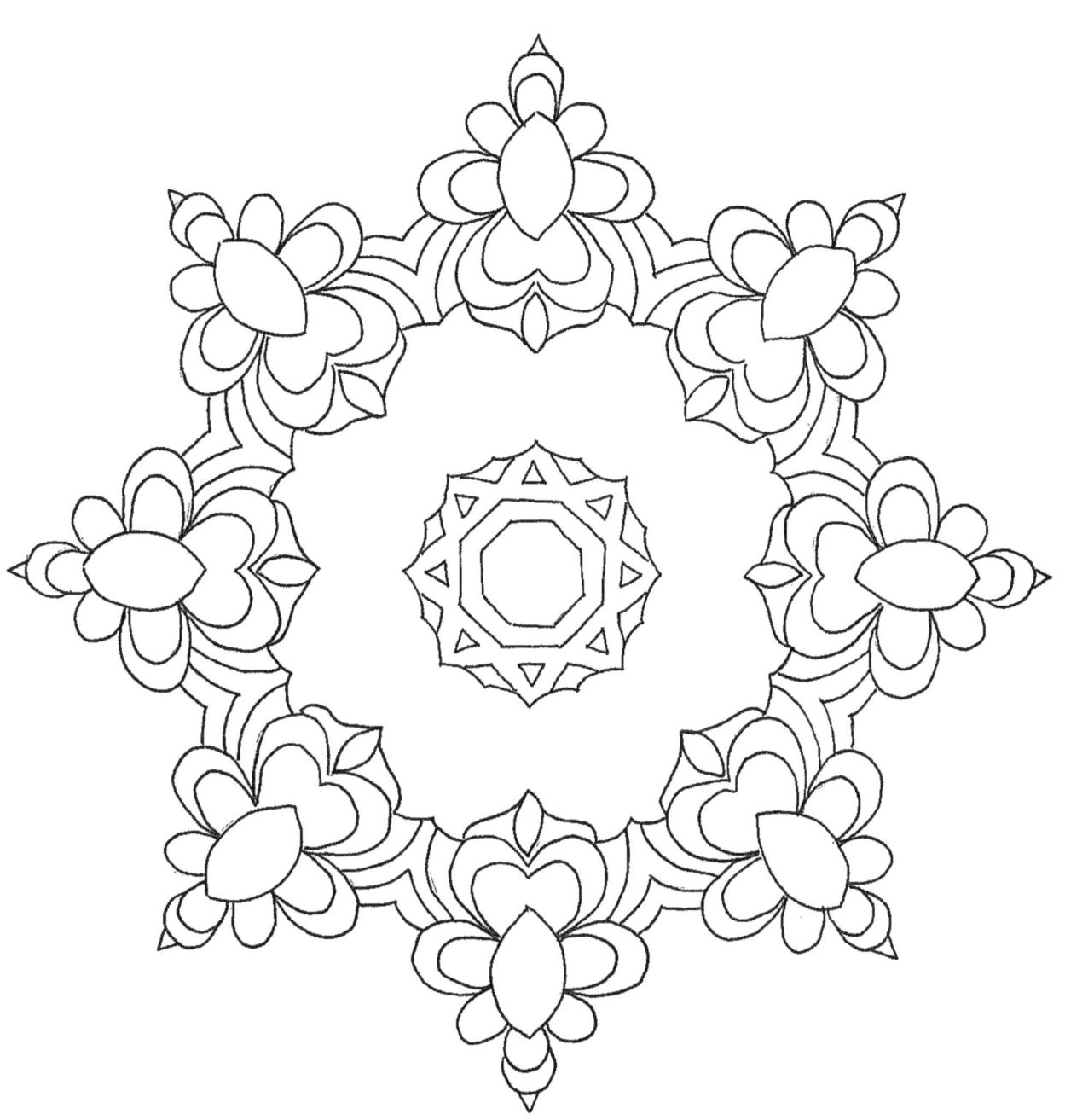

Write in your journal honest feelings you are having right now.

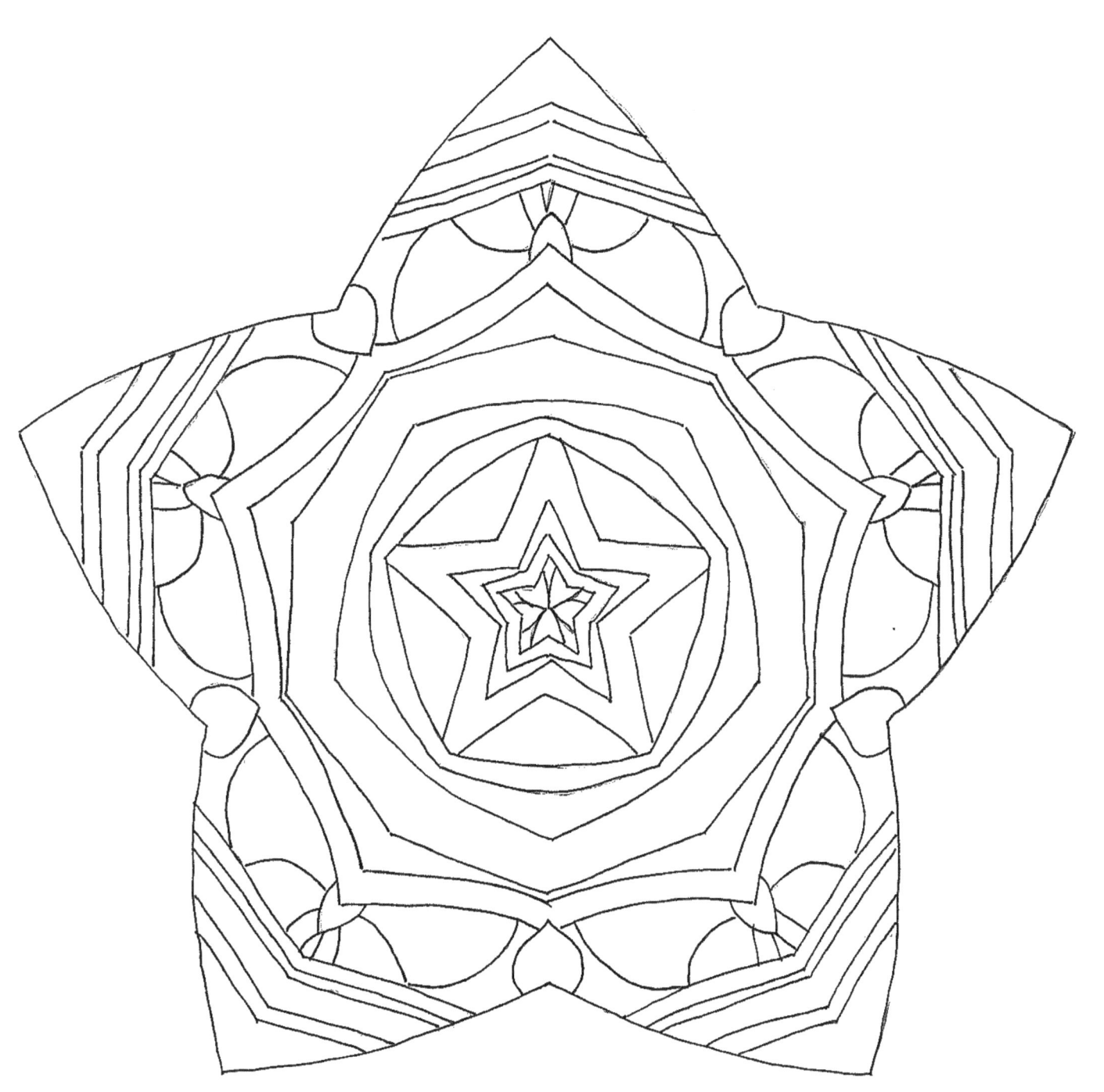

In your journal write things you would do if you were a millionaire.

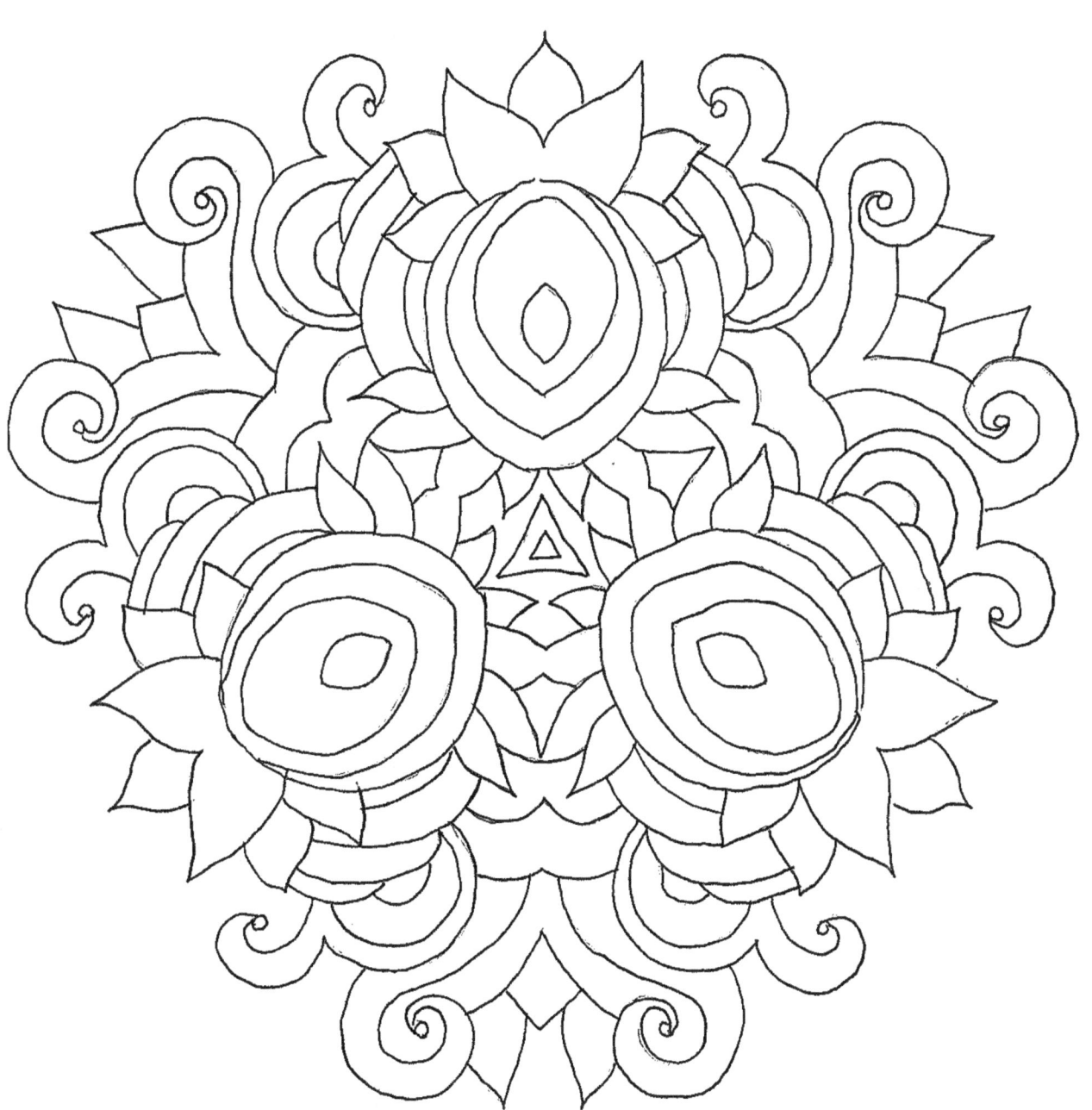

List things you would like to hear from others.

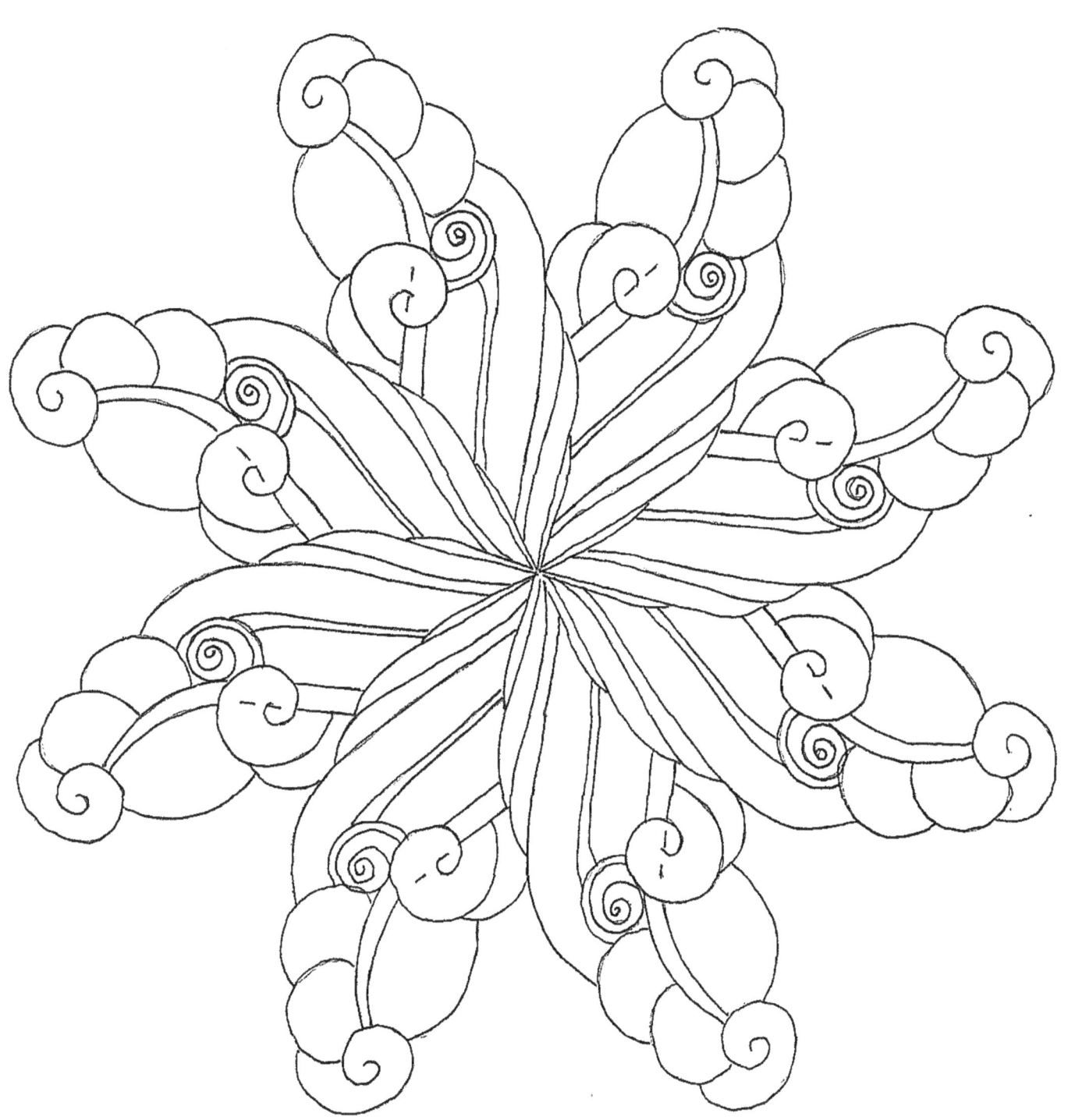

Write things that used to scare you but don't any more.

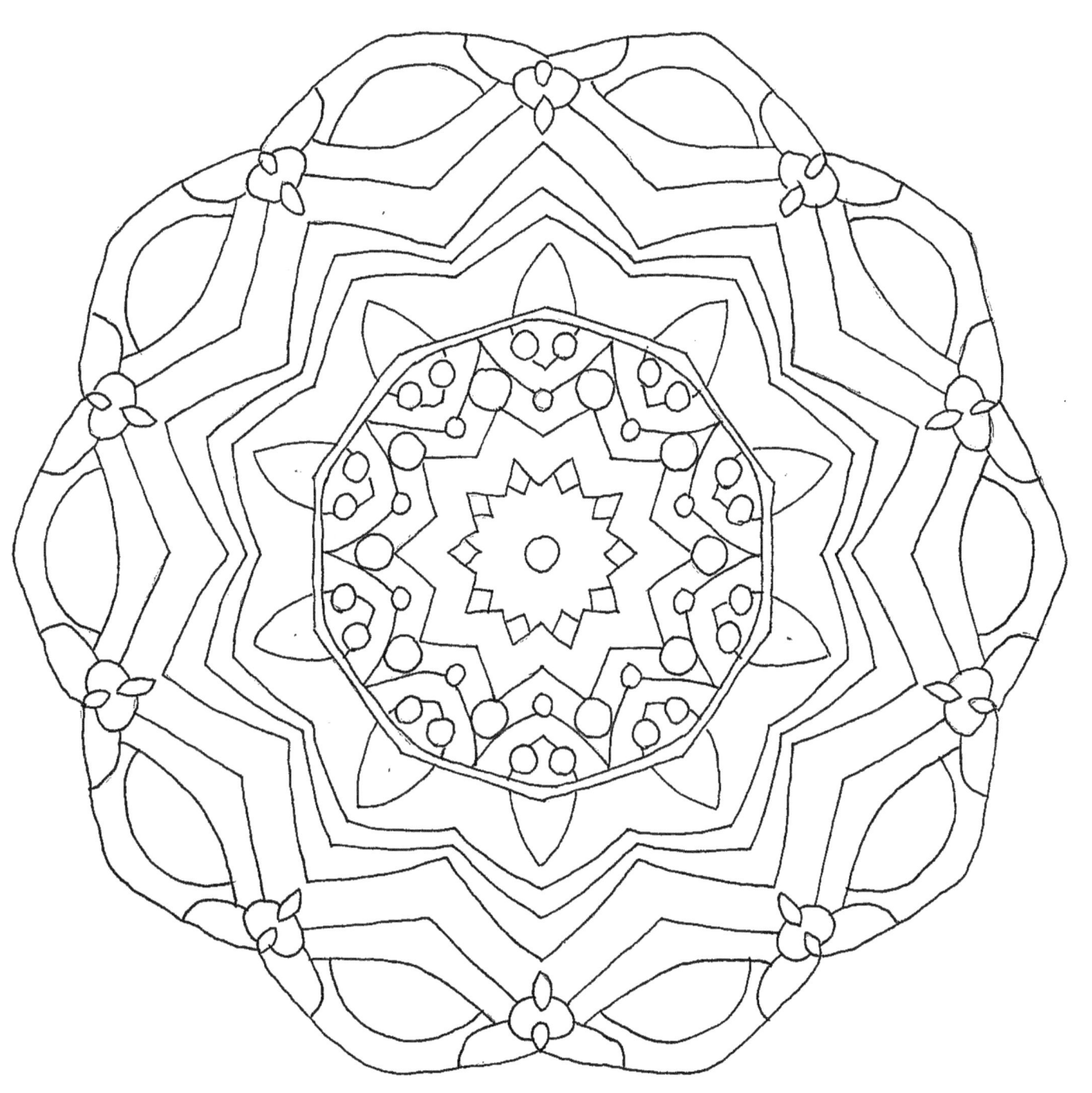

Make a list of things you are sad or angry about.

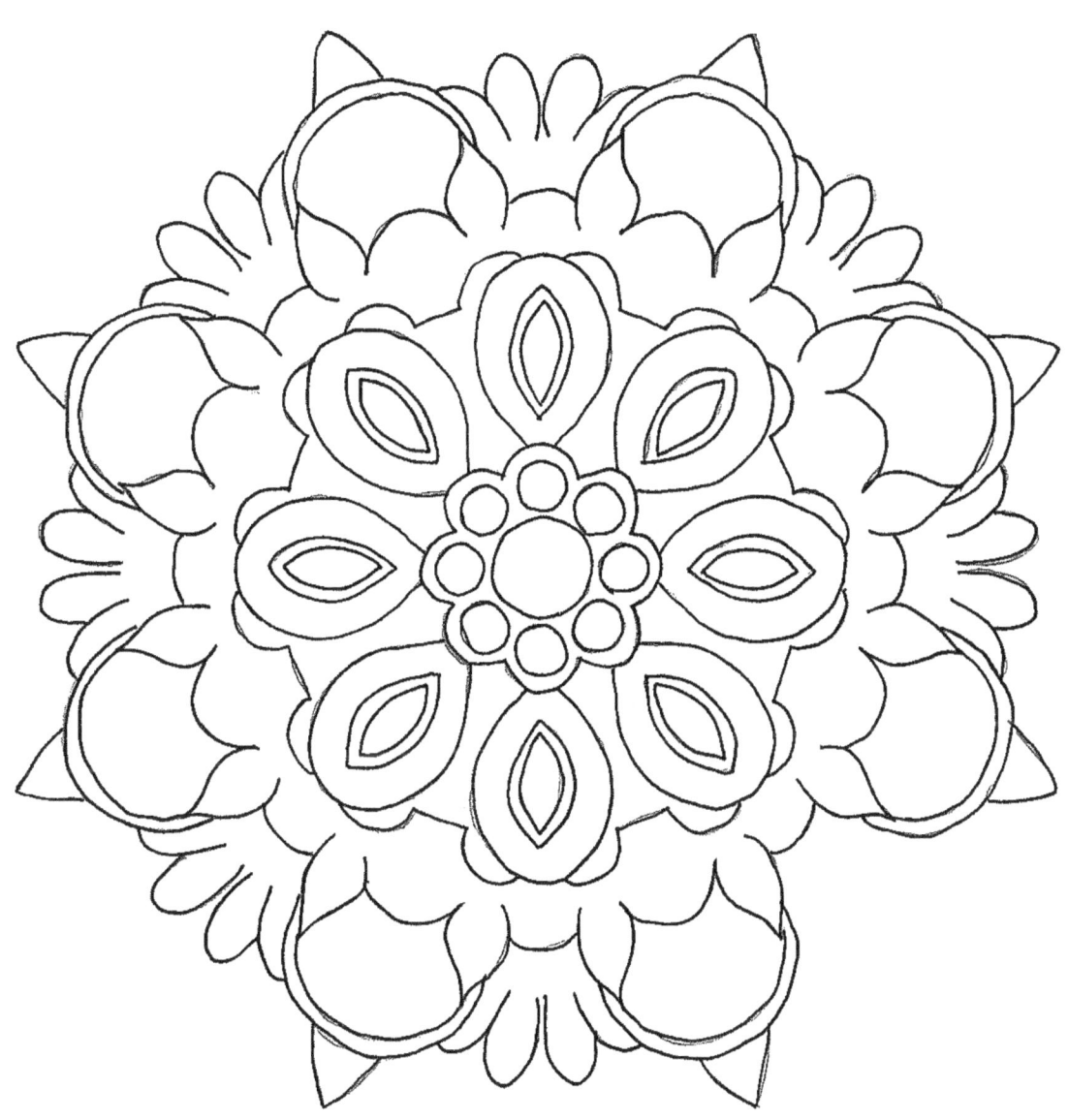

List things you fear.

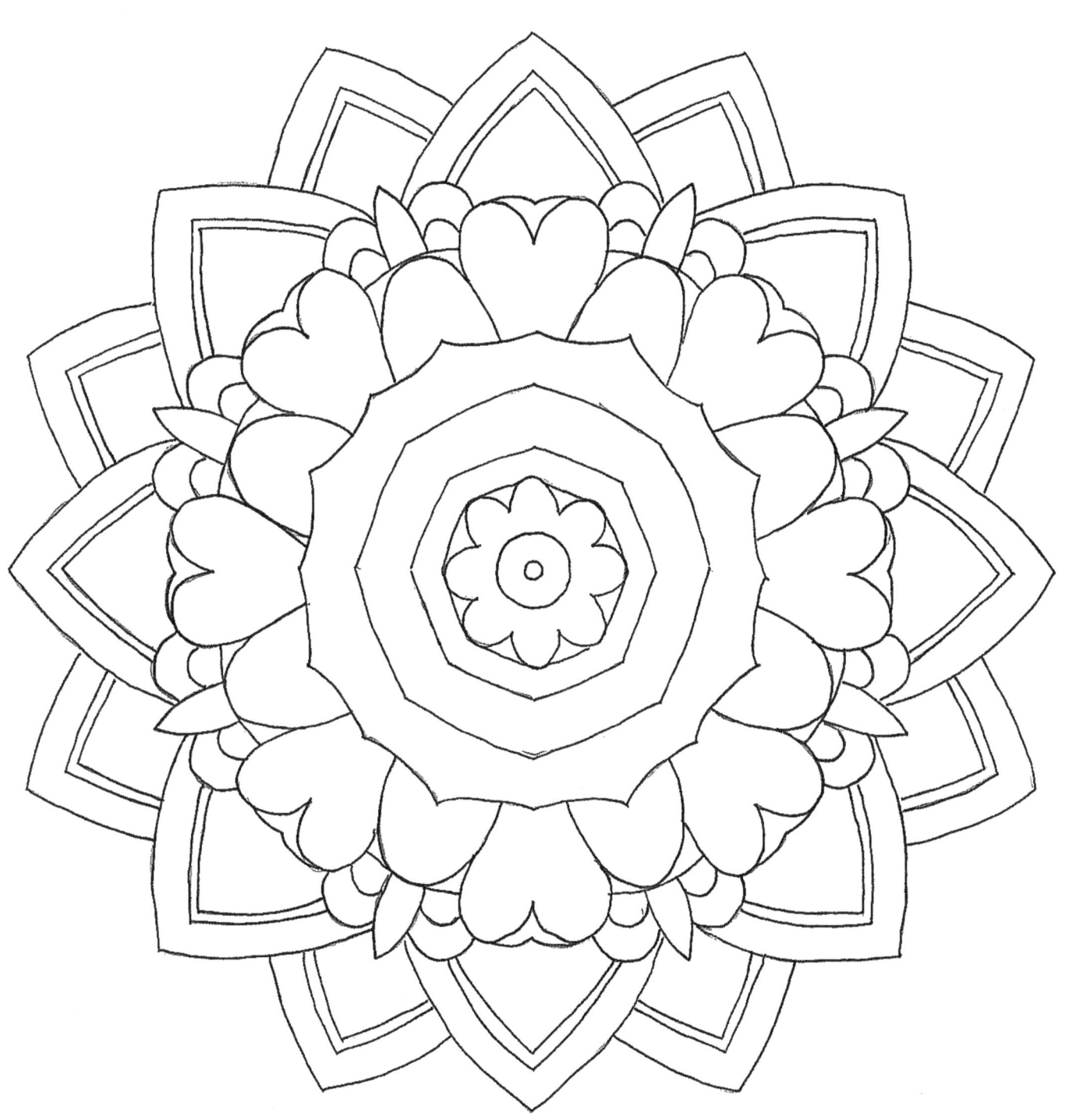

Write questions in your journal that you would like answers for.

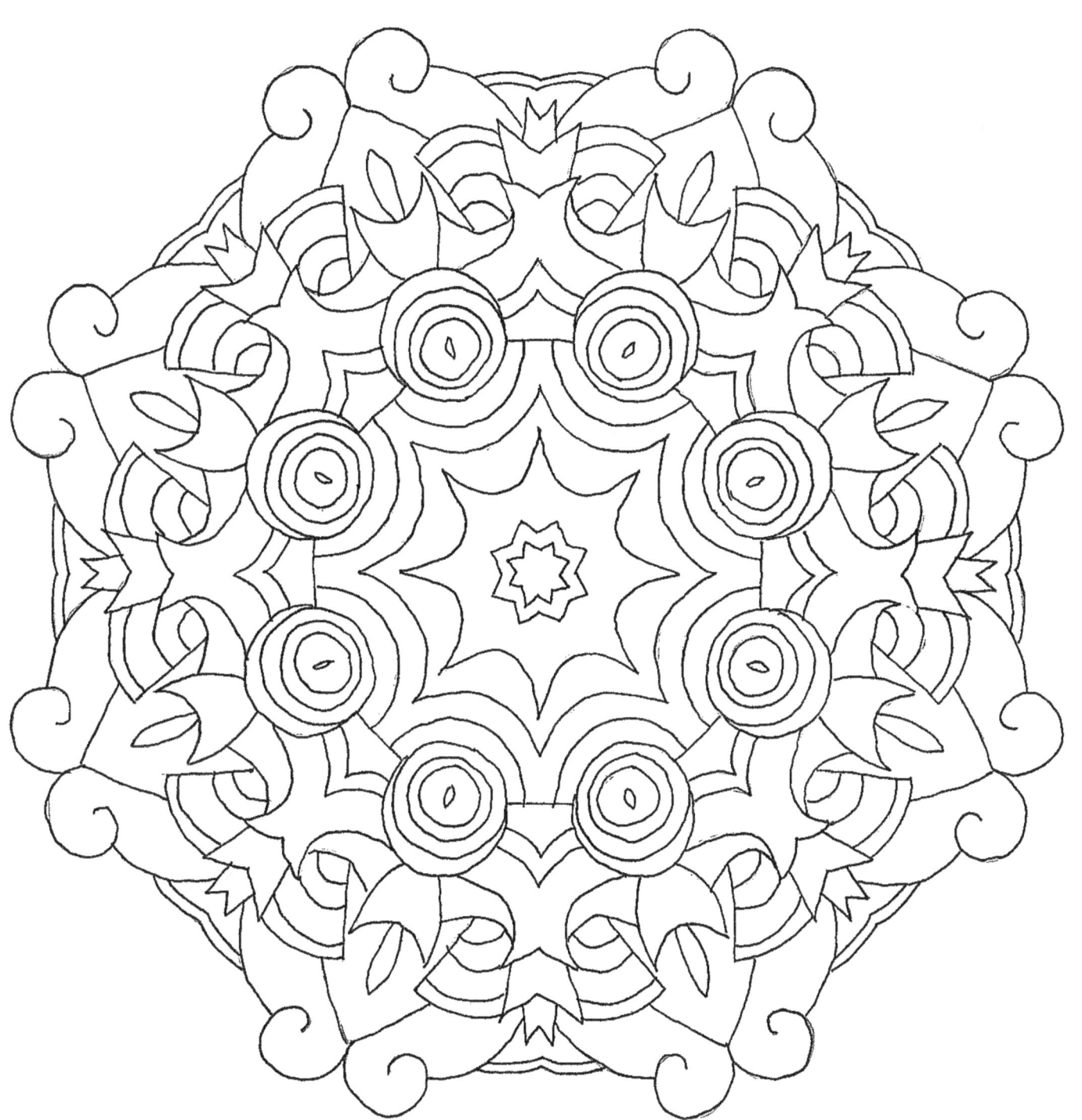

Write things in your journal that make you laugh.

Write things in your journal that make you cry or touch your heart.

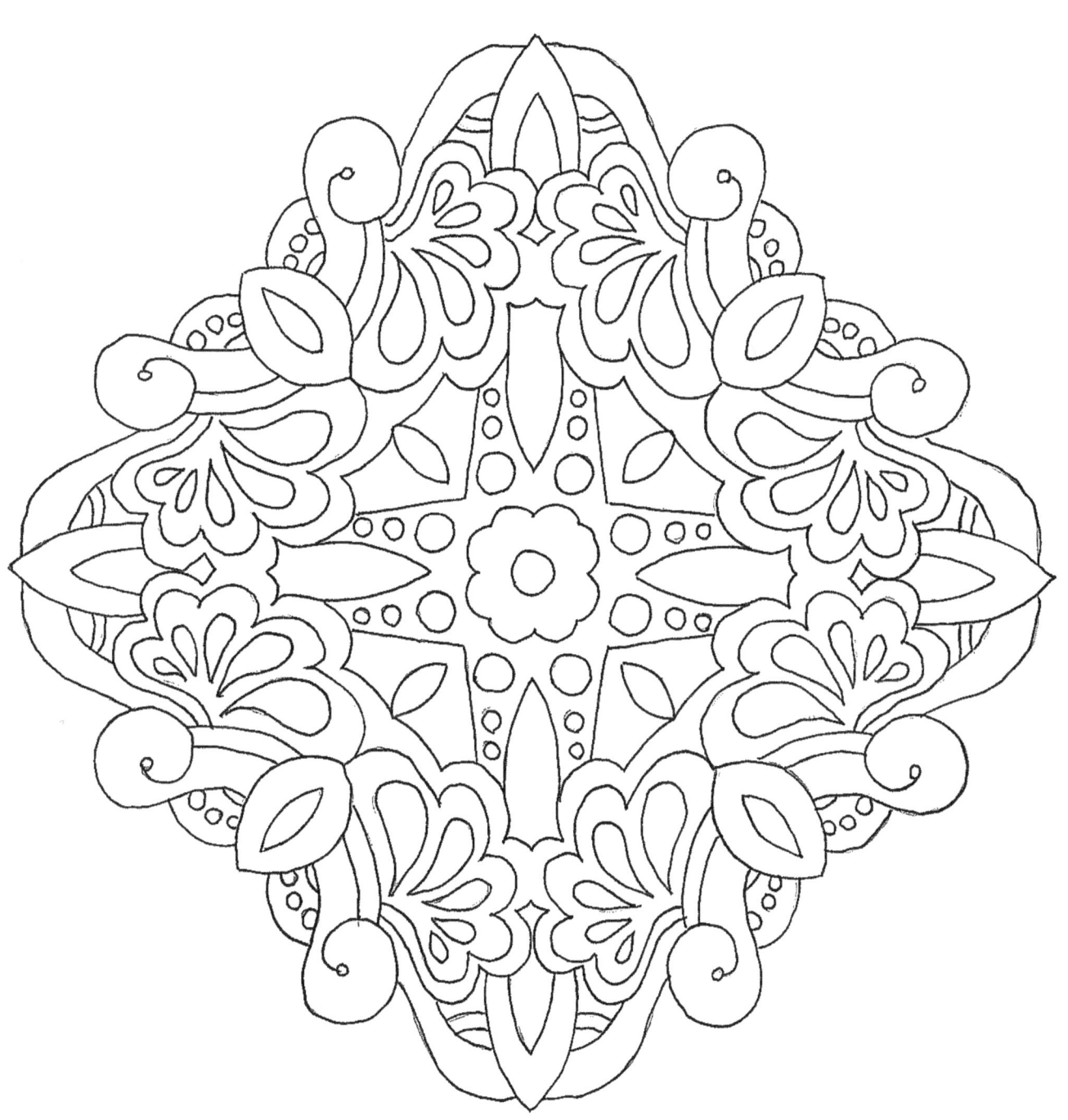

A journal is a good place to list possessions you are tired of owning.

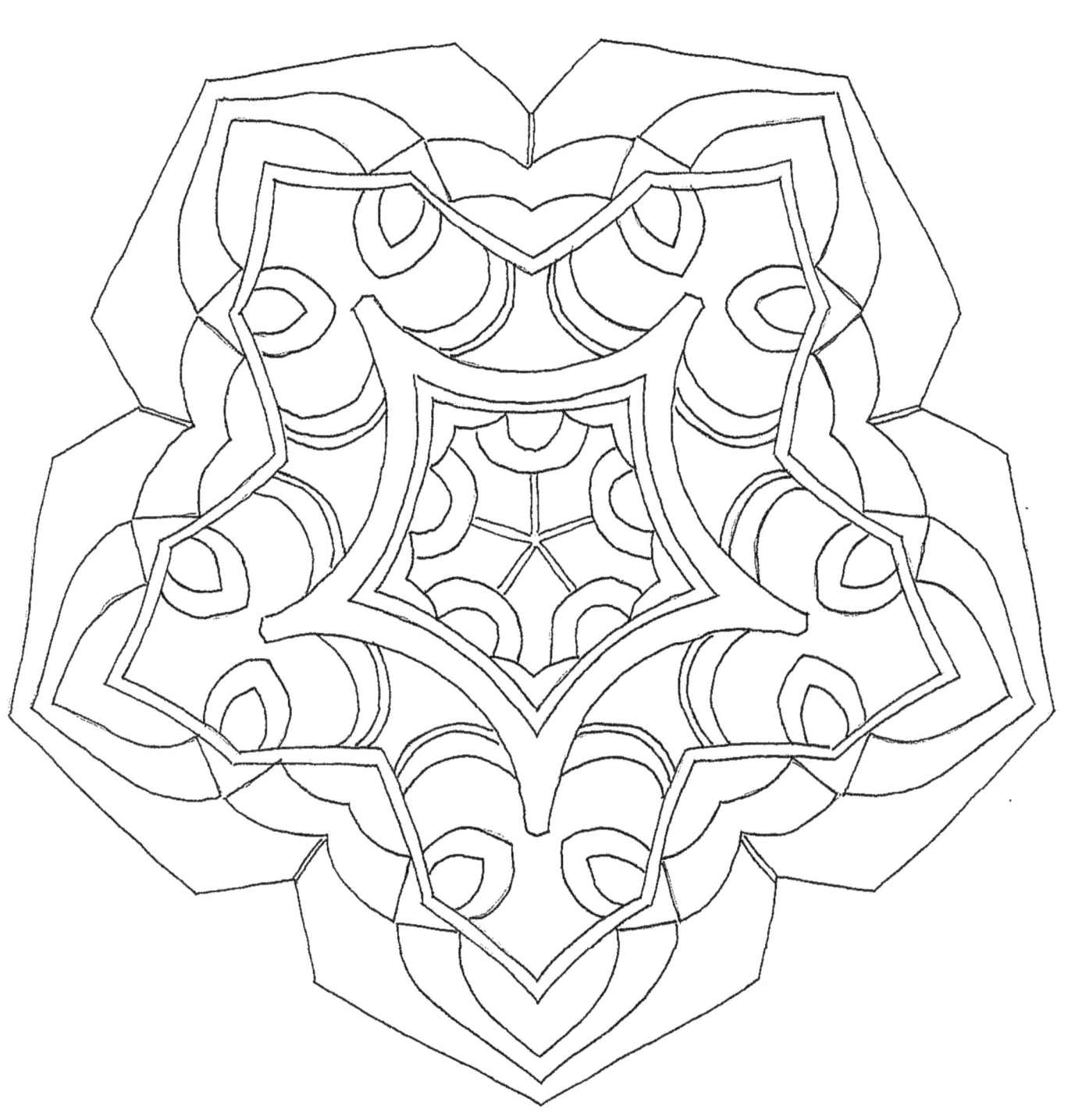

Make a journal list of childhood memories.

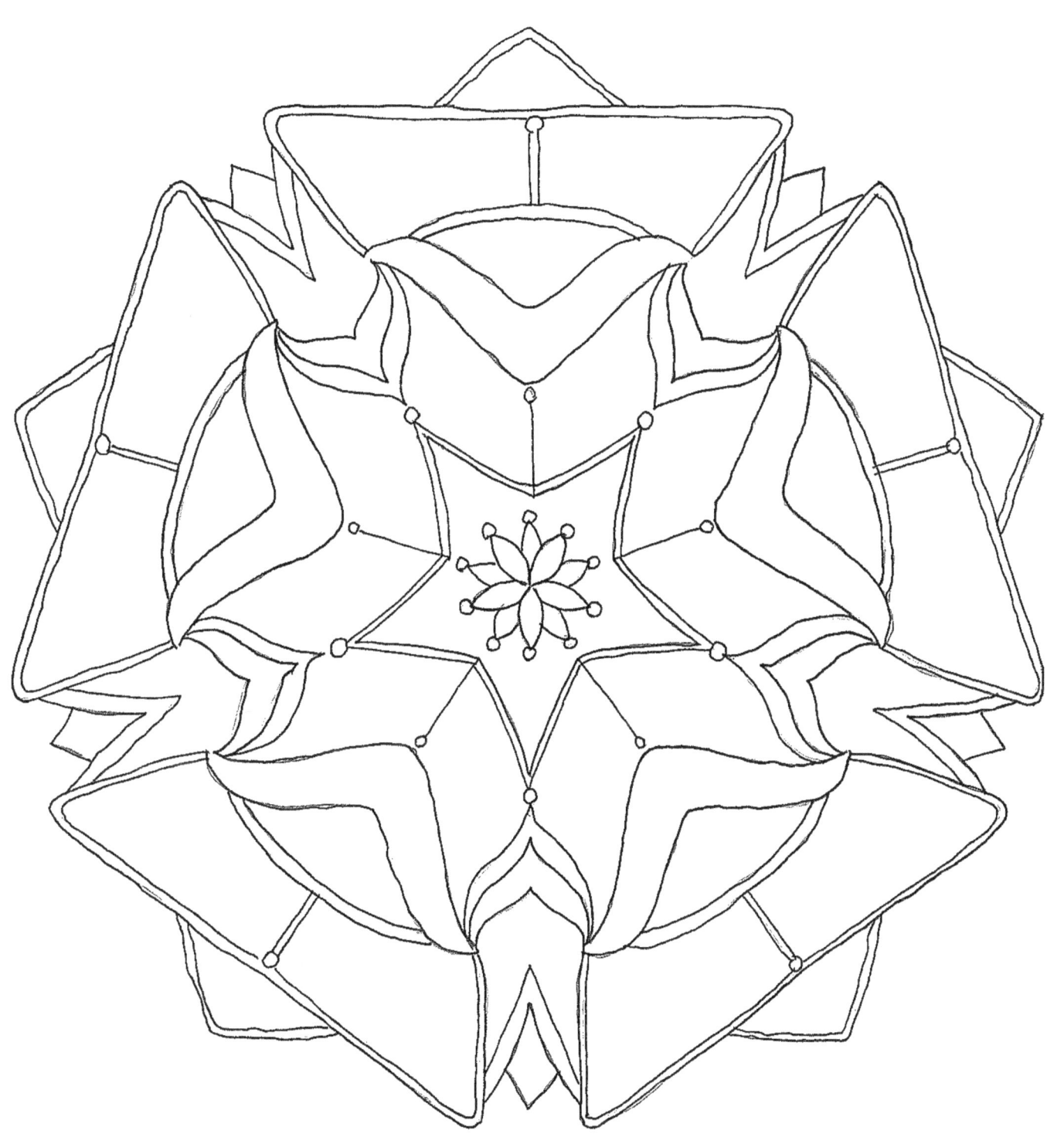

Write down skills and qualities you like in yourself.

_____
_____
_____
_____
_____
_____
_____
_____
_____
_____
_____
_____
_____
_____
_____
_____
_____
_____
_____
_____
_____
_____
_____
_____
_____
_____
_____

Make a list of things that are hard to share verbally.

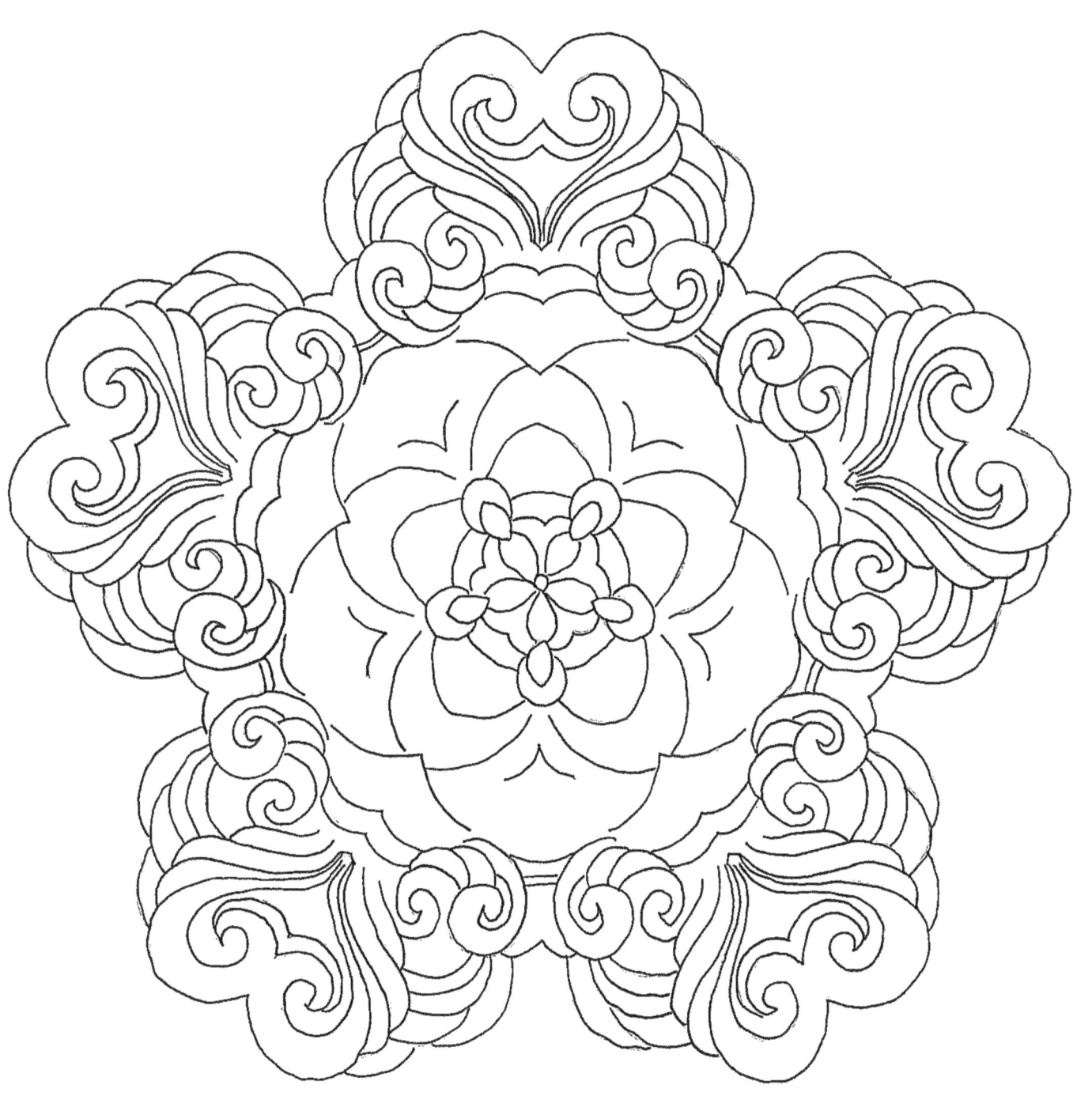

List things you are glad you have done in your lifetime.

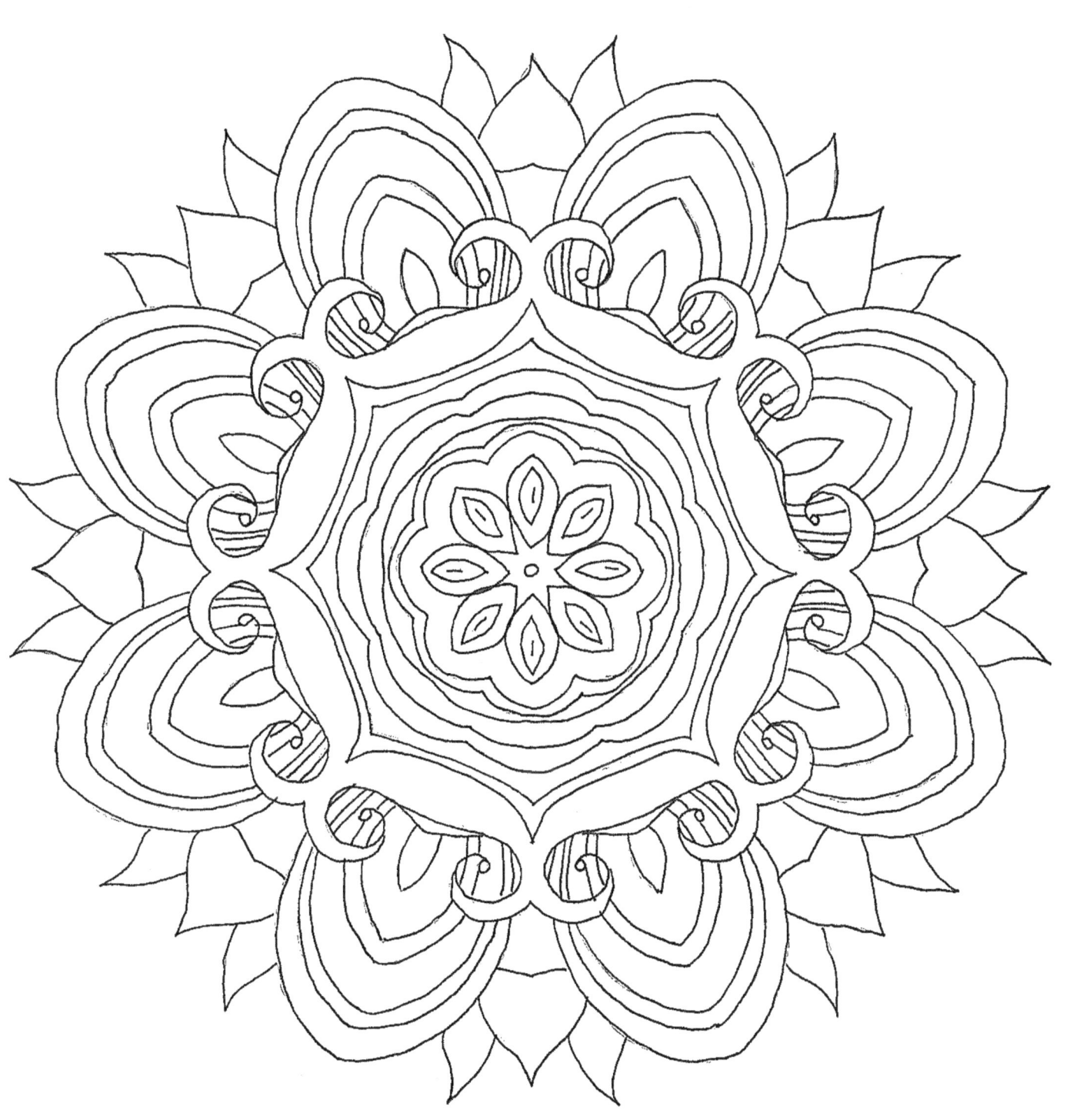

List things you would like for your children to know about you.

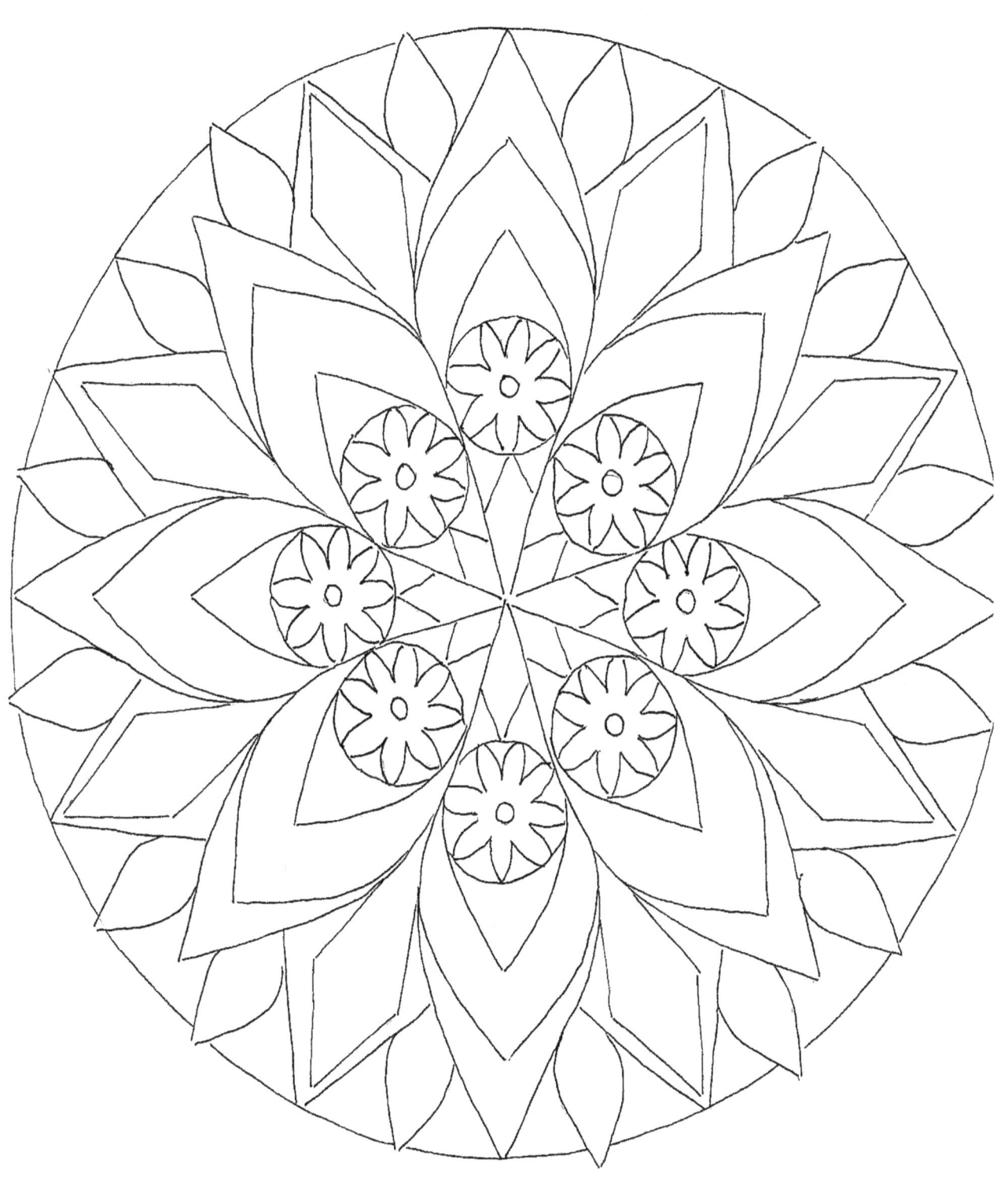

Bees are helpful to a garden. They love flowers that close at night.